Commotion

poems by

Karen Sagstetter

Finishing Line Press
Georgetown, Kentucky

Commotion

ACKNOWLEDGMENTS

I gratefully acknowledge the following publications, where many of these poems first appeared.

Poet Lore, ArLiJo/Arlington Literary Journal, Beltway Poetry Quarterly, Bits, Black Buzzard Review, The Denny Poems, District Lines, Earth's Daughters, Five 2 One, Immersion Journals, Innisfree Poetry Journal, Little Patuxent Review, Maryland Millennial Anthology 2000, GW Review, The Pearl, Tidal Basin Review, Unlikely Stories Mark V; and chapbooks: *Ceremony* (State Street Press), *Half the Story* (Charles Street Press).

Special thanks to Terence Winch, Gail Spilsbury, Mary Kay Zuravleff, and Jody Bolz.

Publisher: Leah Maines
Editor: Christen Kincaid
Cover Art: Copyright Rona Schwarz, www.photosbyrona.com
Author Photo: Kelcy Sagstetter
Cover Design: Leah Huete

Printed in the USA on acid-free paper.
Order online: www.finishinglinepress.com
            also available on amazon.com

Author inquiries and mail orders:
Finishing Line Press
P. O. Box 1626
Georgetown, Kentucky 40324
U. S. A.

Table of Contents

NEW MOON

THIS BUS IS AMAZING

for my beloved friends and family

NEW MOON

Now that you're in a better mood

No more crawling around the yard
No more scattering my diamonds
No more complaining about banana peppers
 or World War II commanders
You can't denounce the radio
You can't say: I'm tired of fish fritters
        I won't drive in the afternoon
        I hate moonrise
You can't wish for pinker tulips
From now on, it's the ocean, infinite and wise
It's birdsong and starlight, 24/7

Afternoon at Arlington Cemetery

Our dad, old veteran,
cornball talker,
stops strangers on street corners:
great collie you have there, your kids
sure are high, wide and handsome.
People love it, or they twitch,
and check their watches.

He refuses to fritter money
on funerals, insists on the cheapest urn, so
his fresh ashes are solemnly interred
by a grateful nation (honor guard,
bugle) in a green plastic box.
He would've laughed about that.
He would've liked the sunny columbarium,
the soldier from Colorado
who in 1945 marched into Buchenwald.

Heart Breaking

does it snap in two
a brittle noise
or is it little hoarse pieces
is there someone who will love you anyway
create a blend of glue and glaze
so you can breathe
on this merciful and glorious day

She Never Liked Communists

In my dream
the Red Chinese throw my mother into prison.
The food is okay, but
she hates it there. "This is awful," she says.
They e-mail a picture of Mom
 looking up from a dungeon.
Their view is: she has a bad attitude,
 needs re-education.
I call everyone I know in Washington,
caution Congress that she is mayor pro-tem
of a small town on the coast.
Her numerous children, grandchildren,
cousins, in-laws are ordinary citizens;
my mother's clan, not to mention neighbors, friends,
and countless shrimpers, could swing a medium-sized county
in a mid-term election. Sure enough, there follow
fundraisers, rallies, call-ins. Shorefront hamlets
and port cities throughout America stir to action.
The president is sympathetic. He reaches the People's Liberation Army
on a secure line and barks *We want her back*
but the Supreme Commander is out practicing his backhand.
My brothers and I check her apartment,
figuring maybe there's been a huge mistake.
We listen but can't hear her voice.
We fear she's in for miserable decline
and consider assaulting the Forbidden City.
Saturday arrives, a rainy morning.
I wake up next to my husband.
He reminds me my mother has already died.
We'd all been so busy but now
we have no particular plans. Without her,
we can't think what to do in the afternoon.

Soloist

Let the chords not be
sounded by a piano
with its history of
birthday parties,
barstools, and
crooners.
And not by a pipe organ
in the habit of
announcing matrimony
or a trio of violins
accustomed to jigs.
It can't be a flute
tuned up for sonatas.
There must be no
whistling whatsoever
and certainly not a jazz
clarinet.

These are not
instruments for calling out
sorrow. When sorrow takes you,
not even a bugle at taps
is sad enough.

Give me a young bagpiper
poised on the banks of the river, wearing
a dark kilt, taking the measure
of the other shore. Let her blow into
the solemn bag until
her breath becomes a surge
of coarse notes, louder, and again louder
and her music shatters the
whir of fishermen casting for bass and
the splashes of open water swimmers.
Let her storm the river
and blast the heavens apart, bellowing
for her dead mother
to come back.

Mexican Feast

Inside the stone chapel
we are longing for you.
Near the pulpit, we spread a table
with photographs: you, plump
in your Irish mama's lap.
You cocking a cigarette, smart in pleated slacks.
You with Dad in church, lace train
billowing behind.
For our first birthdays, you baked
chocolate cakes, and there we are,
each in turn, ecstatic with
cheeks full of frosting.

We sit in the pews we'd dreaded
as dear ones speak about
how you taught us
to crack crabs and play Scrabble,
how you nudged us
to fall in love, how happy
you were whenever thunder
swept over the bay

and now
we are supposed to bury you.
At least majestic live oaks hover
like angels over the plot. At least
sprays of yellow roses embrace
the casket. Everybody's here—
the grandbabies you loved to lift high.

Afterward, we gather for your favorite
margaritas, enchiladas, tres leches.
We stuff ourselves in your honor. We laugh
like there's no tomorrow. We toast you.
We kiss each other.
We love you all over and we are not
saying goodbye.

Heartache

you want to know

is it still tender

does touching the soft bruise

with your little finger

still make you wince

deep inside your chest

Sunrise over the Mall

Your bus stops on a high road.
Sloping below in concrete is the mall—Starbucks,
Safeway, Subway, cool boutiques.
The bus is a monster, wheezing and lurching and late
but the sun is right on time, rising.
Streams of gold light fight through
distant telephone poles and close buildings.
Curling clouds, a stray star—the sky melts to orange, yellow, light blue
and especially pink, giant swaths of it.
People don't like to praise pink.
You look like a fool, mooning over pink,
someone who could never manage money or drive a black car.
Still, you know that in ancient times,
this was not a commuter route
but a green ridge commanding a valley
thick with maples and oaks, weeping cherries and dogwoods.
Dawn came floating every morning, creating wide pastel skies.
Pink was just fine back then.

Not a Harvest Moon

This isn't a full strawberry moon
or a full corn moon. Not an egg or milk moon.
Not a full sturgeon moon, a beaver, buck or wolf moon.
Nor is it a hunter's moon, a snow moon, a full cold moon.
I wish it were a harvest moon, but it is not.
If it were a flower moon, we'd be skipping
on the patio but no, it's a new moon,
barely visible the first night out,
just a sliver in a black sky
until it waxes buoyant and dazzling,
tempting us with the idea
that light follows darkness
every time.

Spring Equinox

Besieged by blizzards and perilous ice,
we had forgotten entirely about peach blossoms,
we could no longer imagine
lazing on rafts in turquoise seas
and bare feet on picnic blankets.
But winter blasts are shifting
to twilight that runs tenderly into evening.
Today the sun is mild and sweet,
coaxing crocuses from frosted dirt.
Light and dark, day and night,
like the balance held by a good woman
in the old Dutch painting.

Summer Solstice

Today, an earthquake struck, unheard of in the capital,
and no one knew what to do. A sandwich slid off my desk.
Plus, my cousin pitched a brick
through the window at Whole Foods.
It's only 16:37 and there are still
four hours of daytime left, six if you count astrotwilight.
I am not looking forward to going home.
The hallways are always littered with radios and tiny bottles of shampoo
and now it will be worse. I'll have to pick my way
through a jumble of sandals and old newspapers
 just to get inside.

If I had a porch overlooking Chesapeake Bay
I could rock slowly and talk
everything over with my mother.
I could hold her hand if she got tired.
I'd be grateful for the beautiful, extra hours of light.

Breakfast at the City Wildlife Center

For orioles I chop grapes, mulberries, caterpillars, moths.
For foxes, it's minced mice, crickets.
For squirrels, squash, carrots, peas—they can't just eat nuts all day.
For our snapping turtle, no ducklings, no frog eggs, but we offer
water hyacinths, apples, minnows, snakes.
Our baby robin broke his wing. He's crazy hungry, his beak gapes open,
he shrieks for food from my dropper.
Baby possums are sleeping in a baby-possum hammock.

These creatures were lost and now they're found
or so we think. Lights are dim, our voices low,
we don't stroke them.
We don't croon: *my manly turtle. State reptile of New York!*
My darling polecat, my busy beaver!
For if they learn to love us
they might hesitate
to leave for home, we might not
let them go.

Someone

Someone threw bleach
at the mother possum.
In the rescue pen, she is trembling.
When I offer berries
she flinches at the scent
of human, of evil.

By the Potomac

Who knows whether worry
or joy stopped the wild river
but all ripples have vanished.
Images of great morning clouds
are etched perfectly
on a flat mirror of water.
No rapids, no drifts.
No eddies. Radiant glass,
utterly still. Except
for the mallard and six ducklings
gliding in formation midstream.
Their tiny wake rolling tenderly to shore.

New Year's Eve in Colorado

Last year I lost my temper at the chickens,
forgot to sweep the porch, burned the onions.
I watched cop shows for ten months,
drove all the way to Philly in second gear.
Instead of chasing foul balls
I just stood there. I should've practiced
my singing, paid off the telescope, sorted batteries.
I'm creating a database
to track my mistakes but my husband interrupts

and invites me to climb Pike's Peak.
Those purple mountain majesties
are dazzling white; the sky, vast pure blue.
If I just crunch one boot,
then the other, through the thick trail
of eternal snow, he promises we'll be lucky
and spot raptors and foxes. On the summit
we'll enjoy the rumble of cracking ice.
At midnight we'll ignite girandoles,
pinwheels, sparklers that blaze all the way to Denver.
He reminds me that regret
is not helpful in avalanche country. Next year
I'll weed all the gardens in the neighborhood. Next year
I'll make it to my brother's bedside in time.

In the Andes, the horses

come down the sky
the pass
a river
they dance toward us
their hooves
skid in loose gravel
their man is running too
running beside them waving his arms
shouting for us his poncho is
the color of flamingos
he burns to reach us
we are working our way up
these cold rocks
without trees without knowledge
our feet ache all the time
the paths between huts take days
that must be a rich man
the mountain his natural home
the animals are giants
let's ride
let's ride

Village Sketch, Nepal

Sun blinks
through cracks in
the freezing wall, she
rises from the rug
where sisters & brothers
sleep, makes the
fire, boils tea,
makes rice—
her morning.
After,
there are
long black
skirts to beat clean
on rocks, hours
at the river
for her to go
from soap to bucket
to river. Her father
leads her
hand to a broom,
her mother digs potatoes.
There will be rice
at dark &
if someone
comes, if someone.
The day passes. The days.

Bay of Pigs, Cuba

A thousand exiles stole over the Caribbean Sea
in perilous boats, longing for papaya and guava, for coffee,
sugarcane, rum, for saxes and drums that limber you up
for the dance floor. For the joy of an ordinary walk
around old Havana. Where "hey mango!" means
you are very sexy. Wretched fighters invaded the shore,
poised to swarm plantations and cities,
bitter to get their island back.
But Fidel exploded supply ships,
captured them at hello.

I see grainy pictures of heroes,
rusting rifles, torn uniforms,
watches, wallets, shredded hats in glass cases,
scraps of dead trucks, shrines to the revolution,
the glorious takedown of Yankee imperialists.

Divers fly to Bahía de Cochinos from Europe
and South America to explore
a massive wall of coral
that you can paddle to, just offshore.
Here I embrace the clear, warm sea of my dreams.
I spread my arms, slide without words
into the gorgeous water, fall back and float.
I dive for moon jellies and seafans
and a deep ridge of mountainous star,
stag horn, elk horn, and brain coral;
and sponges: tube, azure vase, elephant ear;
a million yellow fish.

"No hard feelings," says my guide.
Sharpshooters are still guarding the beaches
in case it happens again.

Checkpoint at Del Rio

Just above Mexico along the highway,
bluebonnets luxuriate in the fields,
acres of tiny blossoms wave to me.
Loaded with deer corn, my truck revs, untroubled.
I love my coffee mug, steaming on the console.
I love the taco stands with long lines of kids.

Border Patrol sirens stop me.
Black loco dogs bash at my windows,
growling for weed and aliens.
The officers couldn't be nicer to hunters.
Please sir, yessir, thank you,
and I roll on to my cabin.

Plump cedars spread green over distant ridges
inviting migrants to march north
searching for cool hills.
But my land is cracked, rocky, tough on your heart.
The sun is lonesome, blisters flowers, roasts gullies.
Citizen or not, native or not, the bleary sky will forsake you.
Sometimes I leave water out for them, and rice.

Alien Sacred

In Varanasi, holiest city of India
we fight through a choke

of scooters, carts, tuk tuks, bicycles.
Huddling in fogged light, crowds

carry the dead aloft on bamboo litters.
They long for cremation fires

along the Ganges, scramble to die here.
We dodge everlasting trash—

Styrofoam smeared with dal,
wadded plastic, dung, flapping newspapers,

rotting tomatoes, humps of lost rice.
Open sewers haul dead dogs and soda cans to the water.

But we're eager for blessed temples
and we step down the great ghats

to the river, twisting among hustlers
and ancient stone houses.

From our small boat
we watch the shoreline, body after body crackling up in flames.

It's a choppy ride,
matted tinder and ashes, femurs,

bits of finger bob in the swells,
make us queasy.

Soot hovers like a bleak enchantment. We cough.
We can't stop looking.

Girls and women, boys and men, are smiling,
friendly cows munch banana peels, welcoming us

to the warm heart of the country
where I've never been so foreign.

Peace House, Hiroshima

We jump off a shining train, step past the scrubbed

station people, and out into racket that could be

any city, where we face a steel crane clanking down

a load, lifting, swinging tons over the walks, over all our heads, and then it's

down and the giant heaves a monster of concrete: lift, carry,

lift, swing, and down. Fetch, lift, swing, down, clang.

Without talking, we move along the new streets—
immense office buildings

smooth sidewalks with perfect curbs and
smart children too, in pressed outfits

in pretty caps, sporting bottles
of fresh water and sturdy canvas bags.

We are American, thinking of ourselves,
expecting them to stare

the way we stare
at each speaking boy with thick black hair and two legs

as though he were a prodigy
ashes in a legend

that form themselves again into a breathing, flying creature.

One by itself is a tiny thing, an instant of color,

but when so many attach one to another in ropes,

when thousands are woven together, clothing the shoulders

of the dark statues, brash, defiant, they become glorious,

the way bluebonnets and Indian paintbrushes rush

to overcome flat dead hot fields in Texas.

Look closely: each image is a bird. You may try it yourself:

cut and fold, your own color, a paper crane.

      the true crane

      is pure

      white

      the bird

      of longevity

      beauty

      gaining in the

      branches

we do go
to the house for travelers
who want to talk about it
we get desks, files
we sleep and bathe a little
our hosts tell
about the half-people they know
still alive in beds and also
about shelter
In this house are sweet
vistas: plum branches
placed in a perfect vase, centered
beneath an umbrella of lantern light
and there is how
the people create rooms
how easily the shoji walls
may shift because the women and men
want corners that open up wide
and close again as they wish
and when there is earthquake
lightning howling wind
the houses shudder but do not fall.

THIS BUS IS AMAZING

Antietam

The boys yahooing
at farm girls on the way
to their marches.
The good plowmen
turning under dead stalks,
traces of corn silk or
the memory of it,
on a gorgeous morning.
What a country for us
to walk in, a hundred fifty harvests later,
in the same September fields.
Thousands died.

Brother is a beautiful word.
I've always loved to say it.

    * * *

I was a girl with two
big brothers. You had the earth's
own brown eyes. You were my pride
in white linen suits,
so handsome at Easter time,
people stopped us after
church to look.
Our mother and father made us all
be in their picture.

    * * *

There's a cornfield that streamed blood
now a park for families
the young soldiers aimed at each other
the withering stalks made poor cover
soil ran maroon with bodies
horses were mules were horses

* * *

Our brother lives under bridges
in cities. We used to be his best
friends, now he likes
booze best. There are people
who want to arrest him,
mother's littlest boy
calling to her on tiptoe.

* * *

The embrace of the hills was no comfort
noisy with horses screaming
the fields could be green
couldn't be green

He rolled hard toward the town river
like a log over and over
We went running for him
interrupted him lifted him
picked him up
you holding his faltered head
my arms holding his knees
I cried so much
they could never make me stop

Kansas

You lost all your jobs
while you lived on that pleasant street,
sturdy with cottonwoods and children.
Morning, noon, afternoon, and night, you unwound on your stoop,
chatting with everybody, quaffing jugs of wine
and jiggers of rye.
Nothing we said made any difference.
You stumbled down the block
once too often and neighbors finally
found you, down for the count.
Now we are here burying you, engulfed
by your drastic life. I hate the whole place—
cornfields, cattle, that horizon.
I hate church spires reaching for infinite sky,
tornadoes. I used to want you back. Now I want away
from your easy laugh, your prairie.
Clearing out your house
is like spitting at a fire. Your animals—tabby cat, snowshoe,
Siamese, calico—leap softly to the porch,
wander like love through the rotten front door,
sniffing for you, whimpering
and lonely.

for a brother

I pitched into sleep

in a bad rocker
during a
night of wind black
ice my dead brother
trapped me on
a cliff lined with
dreadful bare
trees I forgot
morning light
I could not
remember
home

The Quiet

After, I forgot cranes honking in wide skies

woodpeckers rapping

I forgot the croaking of frogs, braying of sheep

the tread of horses in the woods

high wind in oak branches, the splash of the river

rain pattering the eaves

I forgot drumbeats, hand bells

I forgot the crack of a bat, applause

smart voices on the radio

I forgot Granddad calling me *Sugar*

Like a dying bird I tried to listen

to snow drifting cold and dangerous

outside my window

I Love You

Aunt Liz got so big
she couldn't walk
she couldn't stand
couldn't sit.

She required a flat house with wide doorways and no stairs
a massive wheelchair
a lift for dumping her into the car
a bed that cranked up and down.

Before all that, when she wasn't old yet,
she visited me on her scooter. Even then,
those huge legs couldn't take her very far.

Why are you so big? I asked.

I like to read

Grandma says you eat, eat, eat.

I teach English

Kids say That mama so fat she eats Wheat Thicks

*Lost boys and girls are learning
Shakespeare*

I bet you're sweaty

*I can maneuver a royal flush
I win at pinball*

How could you get a husband?

*We like taking long drives in the desert
Saguaro is our favorite*

How can you have babies with that belly?

My son is a banker
My daughter is a minister

Are you lazy?

Last year I read a hundred books

Does it bother your husband—
the diapers? How your stomach slowly
mashes your heart and lungs.

I snapped at doctors

Does he know that you will lose your mind?
You won't know his name.

We were married on a hilltop

Is there a heaven?

Cremate me, for I am too swollen
for a coffin
I want to be tiny fragments flying
Scatter me as bits of ash
Learn to say I love you *easy as air*

We grew up together

Snatching frogs in ditches, climbing live oaks,
a barefoot gang of two,

finished school somehow, married sweethearts,
raised hardy kids,

inched the scale high and low
at jobs, surprising ourselves with decent livings.

In season we tramped in wilderness
like it was our old neighborhood.

We talked everything over
in tents and kitchens, on porches, at graduations.

Why didn't I answer? the day you said
you are my brother, I love you

It was your dad who called me
the terrible morning you plunged from a ladder

I argued with the phone, fists up,
I broke the sky open

I shouted for you, I went looking for the forest
but there were no more trees

Now I speak to you in a dream, but plainly
I love you, I miss you, I love you

for Randy

Night Shift on Death Row

You jumped from planes over Asia
into fierce webs of jungle,
threaded through blackening dusk
quiet like a needle

You'd spot the enemy, communists—
a camp, just teenagers
in rotting sandals, sipping lousy soup—
kids you were told to shoot

Now you work in America
in real prison, the Big House
with driveways and skinny landscaping
shepherding hit men toward sleep

You serve snacks on trays late at night
tending their rabid stomachs
so they will shut their loud mouths
so they will calm down

lie down
so they won't punch so hard
through your stiff uniform, armor the bosses gave you
Watch out

Watch out for the one
who took aim
at his son, the one who
torched trains, who

slashed his teacher, strangled a dog
shoved wives off high bridges
burned churches
cracked the spell of god

Scan for thread, foil, pencils
the gadgetry of uprising—
for killers want to live
and they are more intricate

than you
You're balding, have bad knees
but you step into midnight
keeping proud

You chisel through the four walls
of insanity, hear unspeakable ranting
You keep cool
You do this job

Here is a home for your rogue bravery
where you are not just some clerk
folding and unfolding
your green beret.

for my brother, Leigh

Farm News, 1950

Still night
he'd hold his sleeping wife from behind
those last few minutes before
loading his bare feet on the rug,
before facing the pokey shower.
She said he was a bull in the city,
better learn to hush. He learned
to look forward to making coffee,
leaving her cup warm on the pilot.
Outside, dew on the Ford, mockingbirds.
He'd think of mean roosters
on Daddy's farm, the old milk-cow,
years of studying to get out.
Now the same shortcut every dawn
past the stucco house.
He'd gun it coming off the last curve,
glad he didn't work insomniac call-ins.
He wanted all the working people
to be waked up by his voice.
Hunching over the mike, a start:
the price of eggs at five a.m.

Morning in Rock Creek Park

I wandered along the creek the morning after
a terrible day
I don't remember breakfast
or much about straying into woods but I know
I slipped on shiny boulders and my ankles got wet
News of snipers, starlets, bribes
flickered in my mind but I lost track
I saw a stone bridge that seemed rustic
but I couldn't be sure
Really I was in a plain old stupor

Suddenly a tall man in pinstripes
and red cape popped onto the trail
He stepped my way and offered
a bouquet of peach-colored roses
Thank you, I said
Don't mention it, he replied in a Latin accent

Well, I liked that!
I rolled my face in the delicious flowers
I let my eyes roam around the trees
and guess what! A red panda was clinging
to the branches of an old willow!
I tell you it was not a raccoon,
not a dog, but a *red panda*
Butterflies, too, flitted through crazy leaves
Gracious, I exclaimed
Also, there were dozens of rabbits
munching clover and carrots and performing
remarkable hops across green meadows
My forest turned out to be dense
with sugar maples and dogwoods
and foxes crouching among the lindens

but they were not trying to eat the rabbits
and I was no longer trying to forget anything

Lying

I didn't want to lie so I told the truth
which you hated you became a ball of wire
which grieved me I wanted you
happy so I told you a lie
which you loved you loved
my tongue as it eased
over then I could always say
soft things which I hated I hated
how I loved your not knowing I
became yarn unraveling
down the steps you came after
soothing me and sweet

The idea

that we ever inched
along ledges
roped together, the idea
that we did not
flinch apart

Separation

Maybe not.
She waits.

She travels to China
where the government opposes
the ancient familiar culture.
Still, she is allowed,
she floats through the old landscapes.
They are just like loved paintings
rendered for centuries in fine ink:
karst, river, gorge, bamboo, blossom.
Still there, impossible
to argue away.

Birthday

After we said we don't love each other
I left the windows open and later got up
in the middle of the night hearing cicadas
and other sounds. I went outside where
I saw the stalks of my own daylilies against the shadows

and ran my palms up and down the stems,
leaves and petals hung there
like rice paper, not like flowers, not what
I came for. Just dark.
I didn't know how to begin.

After you left

you came to be alive
inside me. We slept together,
not lonely anymore. You didn't get up
to go, you didn't speak about anybody
else. You were whole
and I wanted you the way wings
want a bird. Imagine us
how we could, like fire,
seem to rise perfectly out of our sadness.

Grandmother Is Getting Tired

of feeling so clumsy.
As if she were with foreigners she could've liked
but doesn't know the customs.
Isn't there anything to celebrate with?
she asks, forgetting there's wine in her glass.

She plucks a name
from distant fields of her memory
and pins it, a weed, on her daughter.
She can tell she's wildly wrong
about something, but what?
She understands perfectly
the quick comfort of medication
but cannot believe the way strangers
touch her now without permission,
is beginning to be exhausted by these people
who always seem so lost and disappointed and blue.

for Rose

For Granddaddy

Would it console you to know
my husband and my brother each
have an arm for me, they
lead me tenderly into the canyon,
teaching me the rivers,
let me take the rope, as you would,
when we climb the ice? Remember
you gave me something to eat
from the sea, you waited while I slept,
you carried me over the boulders, you. . . .

Tell me the story about a lake
in the woods where geese were hiding
and how lucky you were.
Show me with your arms
how they flew, and we'll live
that grand day over and over again.

A Wide Street, New Orleans

In New Orleans everybody drinks too much and that evening
my father did too. I was used to him and went right to bed in our
big hotel room, a clean place with polished floors and a gallery
overlooking St. Charles. But my mother was not used to it, she
never got used to it, and she wouldn't sleep. She stayed awake,
wanting him to pass out and away and keep right on going into the
funneling night.

St. Charles is a wide street that everybody loves. From her upper
window, she saw gaslights shining in the oak trees and she
watched the streetcar hustling back and forth. She sat there for
hours in her armchair on the balcony, almost the whole
night. Then an old black man came along, just walking slowly
like he wasn't going anywhere in particular. He had a patch of
white hair and an umbrella. When he arrived at the tall hedge
across the way, he reached into the bushes above his head. He
pulled a long branch down to his face and breathed from the deep
red center of a hibiscus flower. My mother came over then to
tell me the story of him, in whispers. After, she lay down with me
and slept.

In the Woods with My Father

When I was small
you were never happy.
You made our house roar—
I thought you hated us.
But in the woods your rough voice settled.
You'd find mosses and ferns
for me to touch, helped me listen
for frogs. You pointed to gawky turtles
struggling over the path but floating free in water.

I'm riding my bicycle
through brawny stands of silver maples
creating my own good breeze.
Sunlight slips through the ancient canopy.
A black snake idling in rhododendrons
startles a fat rabbit. I spy a baby owl
high on a limb. I think of you
wading into the current
showing me depth, danger, grace.
I want you to know
I'm more beautiful today than I've ever been.

Commotion on the Hot Pier

the two of us bait up with fish heads
drop lines into Aransas Bay
the strings pull taut
I tug slowly, sweet-talking a big bad crab
from the dark deep
my dad scoops him with our net
he's furious
clacking his terrifying claws
we like him
we like his fight
we can't wait for the gumbo to boil,
for spiced steam, fat bowls of rice, mallets
sweet, hot flesh

Summer Wedding

Little brother, now fifty,
you're holding her hand at last,
turning the ring, a baby diamond,
to fit. You cherish
from this day forward
You love the ribbon in her hair.
The justice of the peace
is hailing the sun and moon
and somebody is flinging yellow dahlias
all through the forest.

The first day of my life

I cried and cried
I'd been thrust into outer space
from a warm red sea
The glare of sunup made me crimp my eyes
Someone gave me a big American breast
and patted my hair
Mercy, whispered my grandmother
Sugar pie honey bunch, sang out my father
Buttercup, grinned my grandfather
My mother kissed me all over
I was admired nonstop, declared beautiful
and brilliant, already on my way to university
I knew right then that mealtimes were going to be great
They told me about beaches and picnics, cars, baseball
They took pictures of my little ears and feet
They predicted the birth of brothers
They begged me to smile but I couldn't manage
It was just a little too much
I didn't have any shoes
I didn't realize it was my birthday
I hadn't yet tasted molten chocolate
I didn't know about longing and gratitude
I couldn't quite hear the rooster
crowing 24 spanking new hours

I Tripped

I tripped
because boulders littered the trail
because there was no railing on the gangplank
I stumbled because
mysterious fog engulfed the city
and I couldn't see a thing
the heel of my boot twisted loose
and my inner ear malfunctioned—
also there was a crack in the sidewalk
my knee buckled without warning
my trick ankle kicked in
that thunderstorm jolted me
the streets were so slick

Furthermore I'm preoccupied
with the national debt
our hockey team was upset in the playoffs
the boss was mean and I floundered on the job
note that I'm not sure who to vote for and as everyone knows
I was orphaned when I was only thirteen

Someone slipped a headset on me and sure enough
I slid into a Motown beat and then got
tackled by a crazy xylophone concert
and instead of climbing
into the bus and taking a seat
instead of unfolding my newspaper
down I went

Still, the white birches are magnificent
with gold leaves, the mountains are so welcoming
I see you at the banquet table
and I'm ambushed by rapture
I don't know which way is up, I try
to sit in a rocker across from you
but I miss and
tumble under the armoire
I guess you call that falling in love

Dinner Party

People are hungry, people are waiting for me
to feed them and I haven't even set the table
I'm locked out, can't budge the front door
can't find my keys
I turn out my pockets, empty my purse on the lawn
I search under the mat and the flowerpot
I can't get to the kitchen where I keep the chickens
for the people who are lining up
My older brother is breaking dishes in the street
My younger brother is uncapping the fire hydrant
My mother is taking a nap on the sidewalk
I text my middle brother, a Green Beret, for advice
but he's busy in Somalia
He tweets: *approach the back door*
I circle around and discover loved ones
who could help me bust in
so I can feed the guests who are starving
There's my father, picking leaves off dead rosebushes
my husband, playing checkers in the tomato patch
my friends are blowing their noses
my dog is barking after a rabbit
I bang on the house with both sandals
my sister in law interrupts, confides that she's giving up sex
will that get this door open? I scream at her

No Crying in Baseball

No crying when I struck out swinging.
No crying when a runt smashed a grand slam
off my pitch. Or when I wrecked my legs
sliding into third.
No crying when I was picked off
at third for the third time
or when my wondrous fly ball
whacked the rear fence
and bounced back like a prodigal to a centerfield glove.
Not even when my mind wandered to the beach
and I bobbled the ball and the manager screamed
get out of my life!
I'll tell you what brought me tears.
I was in space, orbiting the generous blue earth
and pressing my face against
the plain window glass of my ship.
I witnessed ball fields in neighborhoods on every continent,
green diamonds shining through glorious clouds
and dogs the world over
chasing grounders in the afternoons.

Martha Stewart Packs for Prison

She stuffs her duffel with fat jeans
and terrible plaid shirts, decides against
underwear. Adds a baggy jacket,
wrinkled bandanas, any old shoes.
Floppy shorts for the exercise yard,
skinny tank top, big T-shirt to sleep in.
She gathers red, white, and blue sheets,
her "fruited plain" calendar,
a bugle, and other patriotica.
For after hours, she assembles ripe-red
lipstick and ruffles, sequins, garters, feathers.
For she loves the can-can.
At last, a reprieve from gladioli and candles.
Time to read about gunslingers and sheriffs
from her library of Westerns. Time for the
sea stories she's longed to write. Time to
study dollar bills in good light.

Next Door, after the Snowstorm

From our high window, I see her digging
at drifts. I hear
the tsk tsk of her shovel.
She lifts load after load,
heaves piles of snow across the yard,
paces out a clearing.
I hear the thud of her boots
tamping a floor in the afternoon.
She packs snow into small boxes, molding blocks.
I listen to her gloves patting and shaping
as she slides them out, silent and thick.
She's raising a wall one brick at a time
and I'm carried along
in a vision of polar ecstasy.
The mound grows. She fashions the arch
of the ceiling and carves a doorway for her boy,
patches cracks with more snow.

Now the sun is sinking, the roof is collapsing.
Her boy is crying, tired of igloo vicissitudes.
This good mother repairs the breach,
smoothes open the entrance for him, hums.
It's very dark, winter dark,
but the sky crackles with stars.
Her husband calls her to supper, yodeling just a little.
A comet flashes through the firmament.
All over the city, we hear her singing,
a clear bright soprano.

The Bedroom

He lies down in our bed
neighing the way they do
in Westerns during the ambush
when he stands up
he's so big
his big horse shoulders almost
hit the ceiling
his hooves leave serious impressions
in the feather bed
I don't know what we can do about it
he's been there for weeks
do you realize
what it's like sleeping
with a horse between you
waking up with his mane
in your eyes
when he sneezes, well
you get the picture
if you think the horse
is a metaphor
you're wrong
he isn't sex or sleep
or death or us
there really is a horse in there

Pain

I woke up without my old knee.
I couldn't get up by myself.
I couldn't climb stairs.
I couldn't ride a bike or
sit cross-legged in your living room.
I had to abandon the lotus position
and I was hopeless in a mosque.

My backhand suffered and
I was lousy in the outfield.
I couldn't march or high kick.
I couldn't dribble or pivot or swivel.
At the barre, I embarrassed everybody
and had to go home.
They locked me out of the gym
because my squats were ridiculous.
Worst, my mind wasn't mine,
was overtaken by dread
and affliction.

When my new joint arrived at last
healers took my hands and made sure
I didn't waver. I was so grateful, I fell on my knees
and prayed. Pretty soon they were worried
because I was kneeling nonstop.
I loved bowing all the way down
until my whole body lay prone
on the face of the earth.
My family leaned to stroke my hair,
I met the sweetness
of mosses, frogs, creekbeds,
an infinity of pebbles.

Campsite

We could unroll the tent
We could spread out sleeping bags,
hang little lamps in there
I could wade into the cold river and splash my face
I could rinse your shirt and dry it on the rocks
We could find willow branches and build a loud fire
We could rattle pots and spoons, simmer some beans,
stir up a cobbler, boil coffee
We could roast birds
and save the feathers for tomorrow
We could point to Orion, to Cassiopeia
We could hold together in drizzle all night

If the twigs are wet, if our shoes get soaked
if there are wasps
if there are nettles, if foxes raid the cooler
if a band of naked men in bad boots
seizes our map
if rain turns to sleet, if the stars go home
will you still love me, will you let me stay?

The Last Day of My Life

Instead of driving, I take the bus.
I'm able to look out the window
at the boulevards where I've lived for so long
without worrying about cops or weather
or whines in my engine.
I pass your house, and yours,
and call myself out
for misunderstandings and lost opportunities.
I'm remembering baseball games with my brother,
two kids in cheap seats, but we saw
Willie Mays up close—centerfield was a temple.
I rattle along, decide not to hiss ever again
at my ex-husband, but to shake his hand
in congratulations because he chose me for awhile.
I am riding by great old houses with wraparound porches
and swings and maple trees grand with red leaves
and along the Potomac, our own southern river, where
brave beavers, deer, owls are living
among the sycamores. And what about the chickens
my father pampered until they stopped laying eggs
for our breakfast, what about wringing their necks?
How about my mother stirring fricassee?
Where are Grandma and Grandpa now?
How can people just disappear like that?
This bus is amazing. I love the driver,
a young woman in blue with babies at home
who will outlive me, plus it stops anywhere I want.
I'm sorry for the times I didn't vote.

Now we are braking at office buildings, and I spot my comrades
in cubicles, tending bags of work. We joined together
to do the jobs, made task forces, made books,
taught school. I see your beloved faces
and I'm saying out loud *Thank you.*
Did you know that chimpanzees eat spaghetti
with a fork? I'll really miss PBS.
Now we're at Fifteenth Street, Fourteenth, Thirteenth.

Today is my last chance to Google myself.
I suppose we'll reach First Street soon.
What about going to South America?
There is just no way to write all this up.
Somehow, today I'm not blown along by mad traffic.
I am trying to follow everyone's advice, to be, you know, in the moment
and watch through this window, here and now
but I can't help it. I'm thinking again about yesterday,
how I stumbled earlier than usual—it was just daybreak;
boy was I a mess!

But you were there.
You took me tight at my waist and we made it
up the stairs. I think I'll turn around now
and get back, back to what I'm wishing for,
to doze with you the last hours
of my life.

KAREN SAGSTETTER grew up in Texas and has published poetry and fiction in numerous literary journals, including *Poet Lore, Shenandoah,* and *District Lines*; two chapbooks of poetry; two nonfiction books; and *The Thing with Willie,* a collection of linked stories set largely in Galveston. She studied in Japan as a Fulbright journalist and has traveled in more than fifty countries. She was head of publications at the Smithsonian's Freer and Sackler Galleries and editor of the series *Asian Art and Culture*; she also worked as a senior editor at the National Gallery of Art. She lives in Maryland.